2000 Blacks

PITT POETRY SERIES

Terrance Hayes

Nancy Krygowski

Jeffrey McDaniel

Editors

2000 Blacks

Ajibola Tolase

UNIVERSITY OF PITTSBURGH PRESS

THIS BOOK IS THE WINNER OF THE 2024 CAVE CANEM POETRY PRIZE,
SELECTED BY LYNNE THOMPSON

Founded in 1996 by poets Toi Derricotte and Cornelius Eady, Cave Canem is a home for the many voices of African American poetry and is committed to cultivating the artistic and professional growth of African American poets.

Established in 1999, the Cave Canem Poetry Prize is awarded annually to an exceptional manuscript by an African American poet who has not yet published a full-length book of poems.

Support for the Cave Canem Poetry Prize has been provided, in part, from The Ford Foundation, Lannan Foundation, and individual donors.

PUBLISHED BY THE UNIVERSITY OF PITTSBURGH PRESS, PITTSBURGH, PA., 15260
Copyright © 2024, Ajibola Tolase
Manufactured in the United States of America
Printed on acid-free paper
10 9 8 7 6 5 4 3 2 1

ISBN 13: 978-0-8229-6730-9
ISBN 10: 0-8229-6730-8

COVER PHOTO: Photo by Omotayo Tajudeen on Unsplash

COVER DESIGN: Melissa Dias-Mandoly

For Idris Lawal in heaven

Dem leave sorrow, tears, and blood. Dem regular trademark.

—FELA KUTI

Contents

2000 Blacks

Transatlantic

A is for Atlantic, Africa, of course, Ancestor, America, too. B is for
Bashenga: first man, depending on who I'm lying to. A lineage I have
Claimed when my accent's origin is questioned by strangers. The
Door I open to mislead people who only want to talk to me about
Elephants and my English language proficiency. Never about their Black
Fetish or feigned interest in my culinary skills and my nostalgia for
Goat meat pepper soup. You can find anything here they say except
Home. It is not hate. That has no place here either. It is the
Immigration laws. I could go on and on about their ignorance but I
Just avoid bars and dinner parties. I enjoy time alone in my kingdom, I mean
Kitchen. I eat a pound of steak then contemplate my position on stolen
Land. Our labor was forced. Lord, let me not sound entitled to
Money or recompense. I'm troubled by my memory of discomforts I did
Nothing to stop. I let things happen to me because I keep my doors
Open. There is an offensive joke about people walking onto slave ships
Pretending to embark on a luxury cruise. It assumes low intelligence
Quotient for people courageous enough to walk back at Igbo Landing without
Rage. Maybe I'm impatient or unable to think of comedy as a
Silver lining. I struggle to shut my mouth full of wounds. I relinquish the
Task of teaching people to say my name right and inquiries about
University education in Africa. I liberate myself from hate and
Vexations I did not inspire. From this moment on, my
Wish is to seek succor from the stares that burned into my skin, speak
Xhosa until a fountain sprouts from my tongue. Move through the
Years with songs and prayers to lock eyes with a
Zebra for good luck. Then live a hundred more years.

I

Noun

Men have been in the business
of naming things since Adam
named the animals in the garden.
We are men, and on this basis
alone our lord agrees with whatever
we christen a thing. Noah called
the rainbow a promise that the world
will never again be destroyed by water.
Like he knew he wouldn't be available
that summer afternoon when the tsunami
ended many worlds. It is arguable
that our lord was never in accord
with us, but it would mean we are
not his mouthpiece and that everything
we have said is untrue. But we are men,
and on that basis alone we cannot be wrong.
Our species cannot always come up
with new names for creations,
and this is where we fail. Not that
our lord minds. The man whose
invention lifts loads to unbelievable
heights called it a crane. After watching
a herd of wrens circle the dome of
a cathedral, another man named
his tool a wrench. My father,
thinking I will never leave him
named me after a spring. If the bird
at the peak of its flight cannot reach
the top of the crane, it is pressured
or burned from the failure
of not living up to its name. As I am.

Refuge Sonnets

The men who travelled along the Niger River from the Guinea
highlands took from the Tuaregs what they were not given. They
followed the water to its delta where it forked into the Atlantic with
shiploads of crowns, coral beads, and the spoils from Benin,
the empire they felled. Born many years later to the subdued tribe
my father handed me shame. It was his father's and the fathers
before him. Everywhere I went, war stories welcomed me.
I step into the new world and people stare at me. They want
to ask how I arrived here, and if it's true I brought desert sand
with me, but they are afraid I don't speak clearly or they are afraid
I'll ask the same of them. "Who is your father? What did he do?"
So, we avoid each other. I live in their imagination as the wild man
who has crossed the Sahara to take from their bequeathal. This might be
why they drown me, even if they don't, I'll still avoid water.

*

For David Oluwale

I was shrouding the dead by the water where they drowned him.
It must have been a dream since I knew what I was doing until
my father's voice reached me, telling me to let the water take him.
Sometimes I believe I'm in a dream until a cop approaches me
in a grocery store with his gun drawn. Glory to the days I don't die.
I think about the Lagos that I may never see again where the dead
migrant might have arrived without welcome. I used to like to put
my feet in the water at the shore. It used to soothe me to think
whatever washed off my skin will make it to the West African coast.
Lord, I am on my knees tonight. Hoping my voice cuts through the noise
of planes landing in San Francisco. There's more of us arriving in London,
New York, and Paris with familiar hunger. They say the earth is red
because it is scorched but I know it's the blood from all the wars.
Like how the expats who visited Freetown said it was difficult
to watch the killings but didn't say they kept the diamonds.

*

They made their wealth from killings and diamonds. I know I am here
but I don't belong when people pretend to reference the land when they
say they've rescued migrants from dirt. When I object, they reach for
their purses before they shove their fists in my mouth. Then they say let's
talk Kigali and Monrovia. Once, I met a man in the street who said
he just wanted to be proud of his dark skin. For him I brought
Mansa Musa back to life. But the trolleys of gold didn't relieve him.
That was a year after I kissed a woman who is now dead because she
spoke eloquent Bambara. She asked if I wanted her tongue and all its stories.
Everywhere we went they called our accents Ghanaian and were wrong every
time. I don't recall the woman's words but the charge of her voice, elegant
as the musings of a poet. I can wind the clock back to summer in Bamako
where our skins fitted among bodies marching at a rally. Fela Kuti
thumping from the speakers, repeatedly saying "this is why Black men cry."

*

I know Black Africans too broken to cry or speak. I lie to men
who seem to need my help with their affairs. Take the man
on the street corner who asked if I date outside my ethnicity.
I can't tell why I lied since I consider myself cosmopolitan. Perhaps
he suspected I'm as lost as he is. There is a Gambian I ran into
who was celebrating the Independence Day of a nation he was exiled
from—until I ruined it when I mentioned our countries are mapped
by colonial instincts. One time I lost my keys, and it didn't hurt since
I already lost my country. I don't want these words to mean I'm struggling.
For many years, I spoke loudly over people who called me a migrant.
"I'm an international student," I say, yet I'm unable to split the difference.
What I don't mention is the plot to remain here, my mother over a phone
saying there's nothing for me to return to. My father crooning beside her
"tell him to send some dollars, the exchange rate is good."

*

He sends dollars home since the exchange rate is good. His father,
an unpaid professor in a West African country calls him a horse,
which would have been funny if he doesn't work too hard.
He has worked since his first job at the convenience store
at seven. Now, you might have seen him in your neighborhood,
curb mining on weeknights. He avoids talking about money,
politics, and power, out of fear that he might sound needful,
which may cause you to despise him or have him removed. It is
American to disdain the poor. But he doesn't say this except on
phone calls to friends back home who think he's stingy with his time.
He spends his leisure hours making love over videocall to his lover
a thousand miles across the sea. She often asks him to come home
because there's violence against people seeking refuge everywhere
in the world. He stays anyway and tells her it's not a bad life.

*

For Olasupo Tolase

He stays anyway because he paid $65 for a bad life
and a marriage license in Plainfield. At the ceremony,
he thought he saw his lover in the room, crying
in the corner. He rubs his eyes and she's a waiter
who has been yelled at over broken chinaware.
He's afraid his wife isn't smiling wide enough for
this pretense to fool an immigration officer
who will look at the photos for evidence of love
before adjudicating his permanent residency
application. What he wants is to don a suit
and be his grandfather whose eyes continue
to follow him many years after he died in his sleep.
His old hands holding on to themselves as if
excited to be travelling again as he did in his youth.

As You Already Know

The poem could take off
with the talker on
the plane asking
what my business is
in the U.S. Or
the immigration
officer who asked
for an address.
The weak-bladder-
window-seat-occupant
who trampled my feet.
The plane could land
in JFK or Heathrow
and the poem
will end the same.
Depending on who
is asking, I say
I carry home
in my pocket or
in the accent
that rolls off
my tongue.
I confess my love for
terrible bar food,
but I swear
I owe nothing
to the snickering
bartenders who heard
hale when I said

ale. Which is why
I wasn't served
until I left
for the floor where
the first dance is desire.
Me, doing the Etighi
in a white room of
feet shufflers and stampers.

Midwest in the Spring

It is the third day of rain,
and everyone hates it
but not because the floor
is trembling from cold.
I disembark at the train
station into a puddle.
Downtown is porous,
many times I go by
unnoticed—a lonely
man in a strange city. My
apartment is a thousand
exact steps from here.
I turn the corner into
third street. Children are
sledding off the remnant
of snow. Did I mention
it is the early days of spring?
I carry a bag of groceries
with gloved hands past
the thawing lake where
a neighbor's wife fell through.
In a different country
where they say a tiger
is in labor when the sun
shines through rain, my
grandmother has died
already but I won't know
for another day. Tonight,
I will cook the bean soup

she swore is best in the
wet season. Then
I will eat.

Descent

I might have seen you for help
from my affliction with Blackness.

I don't know. Kendrick says
he has been diagnosed

with real ~~nigga~~ conditions.
I needed you to make mine

go away. I wanted you
to will the earth to swallow

the cop at my door.
My relationship with the land

is the longing of my fathers
for their kin. As you know already,

I am not from here;
and cannot make requests

from the land. Your fathers
have reaped from desire.

Upon learning the palace
will have its first Black son

the crown decreed he will
never be called prince

and will hold no titles.
Although I do not condone,

I understand the queen.
The boy's mother could

have removed him from
the crown's household

because she could imagine
him growing up

to be the queen's housenigga.
What puts us in bed with those

who lorded themselves over us
besides our desire for mercy?

When my people knew I stopped
seeing you, they wanted to know

if I was thankful because where I'm from
it's often said that to be kept alive by

what could kill you is a gift.

Forty-One

I blamed the time difference.
  I blamed the miles over
which our voices were carried
  by the phone when my mother
claimed my voice didn't sound
  like mine. I blamed the ocean
between us. I repeated myself;
  but my voice sounded like
a needle. When I opened
  my mouth all 23 years of Amadou
Diallo's life fell out. I didn't see
  his face until I rinsed the blood
off. But I held him even without knowing
  it was him because he has my body,
I mean my brother's body. I hugged
  him because he is mine in the way
my body is mine. I cradled him until
  his eyes opened. I cradled his head
until his mouth opened into stories
  of the many ways his hands have
failed him. He stopped the stories
  abruptly before their ends. He was
restless. He wanted a haircut, food,
  and travel all at once. He wanted to live
all 22 years of his death in a minute.
  He wanted to live like he never died.
But he left me for the shores across
  which our mothers are waiting for us.

Black Boy

I shift my gaze from the news
        to the dream of a barking dog.
                I could not make out the face

of its handler under the lamp post.
        He stood akimbo. The blue
                of his shirt is the color of

night sky. He yelled at me
        until I crossed the street
                into a ditch. It was the same night

I met the boy who wanted
        me to help him
                retrieve his life from a tomb.

He reeked of sweat and dirt
        like he had fallen in his run.
                We talked until we grew bored.

The road ahead meandered
        into darkness. We traded secrets.
                He told me he sleepwalks

and is terrified of worms.
        I told him he is dead.
                He showed me his lungs

through the hole in his chest.
        We walked to California in silence.
                There were two men he had met before

waiting to receive us. They were Black.
        They were hanging from trees in a park. I left the boy

in search of a footstool.
        A wrong turn led me into my
                living room. The news was still on

and another Black man was dying
        on the TV screen.

Commutative Properties of Black Bodies

I chose a bullet as the answer
to the multichoice question

on speed and velocity. I knew
I was right because if sound

travels faster, then Black
bodies will hear the bullet

knocking the door of their skins
the moment before impact.

My knowledge is not physics.
It is Shaft saying "relax,

if you hear the shot,
it's not for you." In

becoming a man of science,
I learned science takes

its wisdom from the street.
Textbooks define a blackbody

as an idealized physical body
that absorbs all incident radiations.

Black bodies are blackbodies.

Which is why science explains Black
death as Black bodies absorbing bullets.

Stephen Hawking argues a blackbody
is an entity from which nothing can escape.

Which by commutation could mean Black
bodies can escape nothing. If all blackbody

propositions are true, it means I,
a Black body, cannot escape insults

at the cash register in department
stores is the same as I, a Black body,

absorb insults at the cash register
in department stores. Stay with me;

see where I'm going with this.
A whitebody is an entity that emits

particles completely and uniformly
in all directions. This brings about

equilibrium only because blackbody
emission is negligible.

Boy

I fell off my bike and broke
into a dance. If everyone celebrated
what didn't kill them, we can pretend
to be immortals. I am myopic, so, I
jaywalk when the woman across
the road resembles my sister
who calls me every morning
from a different country.
As children we swore we lived
in a matchbox, which is not
a metaphor for anything. But
the neighbor's house burned,
and I shot Jimmy, the neighbor's
boy many times with a water gun.
I hated him; his preacher father.
I'm digressing. It's the same house
where my sister gave me housekeeping
lessons when we ran out of water
until she figured she could scoop some
if she climbed into the tank. Which is how
she almost drowned. Given the choice
of anything, she wanted to be a fish.
But we grew up partly with our father's
whip. One half of him planted the melon
seeds in the garden, we argue
over what his other half did.
I think back to the neighborhood
fish market where a lobster once broke
free from the duct tape holding its pincers,

the frantic fishes in the same aquarium,
Jimmy shouting for help.

Dolls

Afraid of getting blood
on the furniture, Yusef
put my finger in his mouth.
We were seven and nine years
clueless of first aid treatments.
He traced the cut with his
tongue. There was so much
water I thought I must be
drowning. Earlier that day
we were suspended
from school, so we folded
paper into airplanes and boats.
When Yusef asked what
I was doing with the knife,
I said I was making art.
Then I was not, at the sight
of the ballooned white tissue
before my finger was overran
with blood. Yusef pinned me
to the wall before lowering my finger
into the tank of the kerosene
lamp. He wrapped the dangling
half of my finger to its root
with a rag from his mother's
sewing kit. The whole afternoon
I thought about my sister's
dolls lying in their boxes and
what their still bodies can teach
about dying. I was not a kid

who paid attention until Yusef
lost a tooth to an infection.
I was scared the opening in his mouth
was a faucet and that he would always
try to drown me. So, I pushed him off
the playground into the puddle. I pushed
him down until he stayed there.

White Girls Guide to Dating
Black Boys

If he plays sports, you're basic.
Better if he's mixed. Keep your
anxiety in check. If you've dated
other Black men—do not say

on the first date. Let him pick
the make out song, you're here
for his meatballs anyway. If you can't
say his name, offer to call him

sugar. Never honey (can be
confused as a reference to his
skin tone). Pretend you know
Africa is a continent big enough

to swallow you. Should he ask
if you are into hip-hop, say no.
Delete your Post Malone playlist

after. Never bring salad to the
barbeque. If you invite him to
your family's dinner, spend a week
teaching your grandma to act right.

If you must train your mom, too,
maybe wait until one of them is dead.
He shouldn't be the first to come

up in your discussion with other Black
people. Delete Facebook photos of you
in African attire from your one year
of Peace Corps. Don't forgive yourself

for thinking you were in Egypt; it was
always Kenya. No, they don't share
a border. Mention your love for Ethiopian

cuisine only in restaurants. If you can't read
the menu, don't try. When he roasts you,
laugh like a sheep. Never offer to cook,

you know you always substitute salt
for spice. If you catch him half nude
glistening in the yellow light
of the bathroom, call him sugar.

How-To

She called me Bo, a syllable easy
enough for her son who knows me
only as his mother's distraction.

I was opposed to her children
calling me dad since we had only
been together for a month.

I snuck in after they were presumed asleep.

Making quiet love made me want
to be a child. I don't know
if her son woke up on any of those

nights but I knew he would grow
to hate me if she was pregnant again.
As a child who shared his parents'

bed, I thought it was the greatest
birth control. Most nights I battled
sleep to see whose need for intimacy

moved them first. Maybe
something about the reminder
of their youthful mistake sandwiched

between them deterred my parents, a joke
I made many times as we made
out by her sleeping son. She was

clear she wanted a father for her
children more than she wanted
a boyfriend, and I was sure I wasn't

done being my father's boy. Yet I
returned every evening like I did
in my childhood to the garden

behind the house where the neighbor's
daughter joined me. We laid our naked
bodies until my father caught us

and her family moved. I remember
the whip wrapped around my father's
knuckles that evening saying *shame*

on you. A phrase I repeated first
to my love when she asked what this
was, then to myself many winter nights alone.

Coda

I slipped in the mud,
and I could have blamed it

on the rain, or the dim light
of dawn if I wasn't failing again

at leaving my mother behind.
When I finally did, she would

say *abandon* each time she told
our story as though the extra

syllable is the weight that broke
her. If I said her tears and the rain

were inseparable, I might be lying.
The night before I left her,

she was praying all roads return
me to her. That night and this

night are the same. The birds
have flown, and the stillness

we mistake for serenity has
descended upon the earth

of my new city. I am leaving
a woman who claimed I was

the first man she ever loved.
Many times, she said I was a good

man save for the one time she called
me a slut. Tonight, we are eating baby

carrots in Vilas Park. I am waiting
for an unknown animal to pull

either of us into the darkness.
An end to the story more convenient

than me leaving at the first sign
of daybreak. If I could, I will start

again in the womb as a child not
in a rush to meet his future. I will lie

to my mother that I am content with
the smell of salt from the sea.

Victoria Island, Lagos

I feel them tugging at my towel on the beach:
these ghosts whose city fell after the first
anchoring of ships. Now they return
in the eyes of perched swans.

*

The houses on the shoreline are white.
Consulates. Hotels. In one, people shake hands
and smile. The Head of State dies in another.

*

Night. There is a party on every street
corner, even the dead cannot stop loving us.

*

Night is a way out of the city.
Money changes hands, and a man is being led
down a dark alley. I, too, pay for sex.

*

The ideal language is elegance. Here,
we do not say thieves,
we say fine boys.

*

A taxi driver once told to me
I have to ignore the city's history
to love it. It was a wet day, blood trickled
down the windows of the taxi.
The rain sounded like a cry.
I cursed the driver's smile.

The night fine boys visited my house
my mother stared at their guns
as if she has never seen one before.
They forgot to conceal
the Nigerian Police Force imprint,
or they did not care.

*

The Third bridge connects the island
to the mainland. The First bridge is debris,
the second is a dream.

*

Motorcycles are prohibited.
Executives escape the traffic in boats.
In a gridlock, I say *home* when I mean *pain*.

*

This is the kingdom of Nigerian Princes.
It is also the city of jungle justice.
The native word for *burn* is the same as *dance*.

*

The urban sprawl is bridled
by the temperament of rains.
Its residents desire gills in the wet seasons
when their houses become aquaria.

*

They are back now with the rains, the swans,
spreading their wings like wet parchments.
Their heads droop as though they have lost their songs.
They look like a sea with no tide.

II

Badagry

[Fúnmiláyọ̀]
Lagos, port of origin from which your mother was missing until
she surfaced in the lagoon, and again, in the city under the rock.
You, child named after the possible joy of a mother who escaped
slaver's bay, in your travel might have met a child of the Morgan or
Taylor who owned your mother. Perhaps he is an educator like you.
You and he, ignorant of your relation, drinking black tea from black pitchers.

[Abigail]
Friend of all our mothers. Property of Taylor, Miller, and Brown.
First named for proximity in sound to birthname, Àbíkẹ́. Then Frances,
named after the ship's port of origin. Then Dead Frances, this time for the dark
soil of her skin. Her war was to stand alone in the glory of the morning
light but the broken bones of her back kept her in the earth.

[Thomas]
Father Thomas saved our ancestors in the name of his lord. I want him
undead and locked up. I want his favorite students from his boys only
missionary school returned from England. I want his hands away
from their thighs. I want to meet him in 1842, to say "Thomas,
don't wear a cassock."

[Ransome]
Named after unpaid fee because captors don't own the land or
what lies therein. Named for the death in your pocket. A name
whose origin you've claimed embarrasses you. If allowed,
you will gouge the eyes of the one who made you a subject of the empire.

[Crowther]
Any position regarding a slave master's name is political. To take one
is to deem oneself an equal. To reject is to resist what exactly,
if you've lost all ties to home? It's ancient wisdom that distress awaits
the child who strays too far from home. But nothing is said of the child
whose home is razed. For you, I'm asking, who rewards hungry children?

[Kúti]
A prophesy that you will not die. Named so because the children
before you are dead. Their bodies were burned as offerings
to the god of your fathers. This name can also be a plea for
you to not leave me alone with the empty room of your body.

[Ṣóyinká]
Son of many wizards. You rewrote the books of our masters.
This time we have names that don't mean darkness. For twenty years
of rain, I have worked your name into a prayer that keeps me during
the storm. I have slapped clay into the face of your effigy. Wake up. Roar like a god.

[Mọremí]
You imagine that the world is yours, too. That you could step
into the light. The world closing in on you, until it feels like a womb.
You have fought for your share of plum. You have won a space by the fire.
But who will sit with you? Who will watch you when you sleep?

[Efúnṣetán]
There are no flowers for the custodian of death
murdered by slaves. I have no problem with your being left out
of the books. Your erasure is a kind of silence. The bodies
of 41 severed heads remembers how they break from a falling
machete shining in the light of dawn.

Àbíkú: Sickle Cell Disease

Kúmápàyí. Dúrósinmí. Málomó. So many names. So many graves
for dead children. How do I say at ten I had more friends among the dead
than the living? So, I say the children of my neighborhood houses
are extinct. Or my mother prays I don't die in three languages.

[Hubert]

I imagine you working on a dance. But you are dead,
and the drums have stopped. You have joined the horizon,
which is why I have seen the air wave its hands of leaves and tree branches.
I have seen lakes shimmering in daylight. Some say these are
signs of your visit. Some cry superstitious. What do you believe?

Sonnet for the Lampedusa Disaster

On 13 October 2013, a boat carrying African refugees sank
off the island of Lampedusa. Over 300 people died.

It does not vex me that dead men walking through my poems choose to speak.
Broken windpipes be damned, I want them to sing the dust in their throats.
They cough. They thank me and say, "we live here now." This is not to say
I am a groundskeeper, or my poems are graveyards. I make room. Disgruntled.
They have come with me on the bus to see the city. Passersby hurry past me
when I claim to talk to the dead only I can see. To them I point at the coast and
say "you would have loved it all—the church bells, open markets, and the beach."

Say you would have loved it all, the church bells, open markets, and the beach
where I claim to talk to the dead only I can see. To them I point at the coast since
they have come with me on the bus to see the city. Passersby hurry past me.
I am a groundskeeper, or my poems are graveyards. I make room. Disgruntled.
They cough. They thank me and say, "we live here now." This is not to say
broken windpipes be damned, I want them to sing the dust in their throats.
It does not vex me that dead men walking through my poems choose to speak.

Justice

For Aluu four

When the stones fell
over him that October
morning, he imagined
his head was stronger.
The other boys widening
the gap between them.
He wasn't scared at first.
He heard what sounded like
a friend calling him by his nickname,
"chief, chief, chief," which might
have been why he stopped until
the mob closed in, and he heard
"thief, thief, thief." When the planks
hit him, his legs
left him. There was a ringing
then a song like a war
cry playing in his head. The
other boys were running
past the bakery when the mob
cut them off. They were
hounded because they were careless
debt collectors or because
they stole from a convenience
store. The touch of gasoline is cold
and comforting before the matchstick
is struck. The tires hanging from
their necks. I looked. Everything
I saw ruined my sleep a decade later
when turning in my bed

brought me back to my college dorm
in Nigeria. Me and my friends were
watching a cellphone video of four boys
burning extravagantly before sunrise.
We didn't talk much after it was over,
and I went back to bed intending
to wake to a different morning.

New Year Problem

Everyone wrote Y2K to mean the year two thousand.
I could have pretended to be confused since I was six
and we wrote '96 for the year the Olympics was held
in Atlanta regardless of the Centennial Park bombing.
I celebrated with dread that the next contest would be
in 2000. We were scared of the new millennium because
computers will confuse '00 for any period in time or
we could be visited by the disasters of the previous
century. There was the great war and the flu in the early
years of the last century. We could be wrong to think
of this as bad luck rather than our inherent disposition.
As we transition into this new year grieving our dead
from the virus, an army is positioned for a takeover
somewhere in the world. I am uninterested in armies,
bombings, and medals but the soldier who will die before
he fires his rifle; and the athlete rendered invalid before
the Olympic games. The privacy of their losses in a world
that goes on and on. I know how it feels. My home was robbed
on the first day of the century. Everyone was busy
watching fireworks, they failed to notice my sister had no shoes.

Break Out

My sister was the first to hate
our father who lied to us
before he left. Hating him
was a tough job she couldn't get
away from. At a bus stop
she pretended not to know
the man whose face is half
of hers. She calls him
your father as if a pronoun
can make him more mine
than a missing sock
wants to be mine.
Neighbors who have seen
him might have mistaken
him for a lawyer
working out of his car.
He wore a suit in his sleep
behind the steering wheel.
They let him stay
in the neighborhood
until he moved out of town.
He allowed himself into the house
when we were away. Once,
my sister caught him
emptying our leftovers
into a plastic bag.
He looked like he wanted her
to ask how he was doing
but a year had passed

since he left and they had
perfected treating each other
as strangers. I wish I ran into him,
I would have hugged him
until he felt shame.
I told my sister this, and she said
you are still your father's son.
It's been many years since my father left
and I have moved from the city
where I loved him,
I still hear his car engine
roaring to go into the morning fog.

High Water

My father lived in a small town
known for floods. I saw it once,
the swollen ground his hands pushed
rice seeds into. He planted with
the care of a naturalist feeding
the earth. I wondered what use
the habit of cultivating land
before a flood is. The town
looked like the closing scene
of an apocalyptic movie. There
were few people looking around
what was left of the fish market
and the grocery store, which
was as old as the town. After
the flood receded, my father's
life seemed ruined. There was
a pool in his living room.
It was a world of tadpoles
and dirty foam that rode
the sea waves. His possessions
floated around us. We sat on
armchairs that rose out of the pool
like little islands. He did not speak
to me until my mother came
to get me. He lulled his head back
and his mouth was half opened
like a toad out of a pond.
His congealed oatmeal was
on the coffee table.

It was a cold night. I was young
and could not have imagined
a hell that burned with silence
and water. Baptism is the closest
I have been to drowning. That
October afternoon I knew
my father was sinking,
he needed to shut his mouth to stay alive.

Brotherman,

this life no balance. Person wey chop
say na god. Hungryman no got fit stop
to complain. Pikin wey no suffer think say him wise.
Abeg who teach am? If life do am, him go surprise.

Na the story for we country. Dem kill man
put for road. Police say na robber. Na we sabi
who he be, wetin he carry. He no thief pass woman
heart with him dada hair. Na person daddy

lie down for street so. The pain pass my power.
I try hol' am. I no fit. Water wey pour for my eye
reach to baf. Police say make we no waka for late hour.
Say dem go kill us finish. Remember say all die

na die. Make we arrange for street to talk as the matter
be for we body; before everything turn yam, pepper, scatter, scatter.

Kalakuta Show

18 February 1977

The spark from the cannister,
a false light of dawn,
woke me. I moved through smoke
like a ghost moves through cloud
to a heaven with no angels.
The house transformed into a battlefield.
My tears were muffled but the soldiers found me,
beat me until I fell into midmorning.
The accordion of my lungs was compressed
and released to a rhythm made by their feet.
They wore masks dark enough to blind them.
They were looking for me, but I did not say
I was the one under their boots.
They herded to the second floor like zombies,
threw my mother out the window.
Her arms were outstretched in the mud
like a child asleep in a playground.

Heritage Park

He was nothing like his photo
from my birthday.
He stood straight, as though
he could resist the years
from bending him. When
he arrived with his forlorn
eyes, I couldn't tell
he was the man who
named me. The man
who I knew only by voice
walked across the park.
He dragged a leg
behind him. He said
work kept him away.
I imagined him with
a cup in hand,
dragging his bad feet
after pedestrians
who have given him
money as if giving them
a show for what they paid.
I imagined him in
a studio apartment
littered with takeout
boxes. He tried
to impress me with talks
of a concert he will
be opening. He wore a suit and
a clean shave, he put a hand

on his shirt stain, he looked
away when he twitched.
Before he left, he said "you
will always be my boy."
He feigned a hook
with his left hand,
and I wanted him
to topple as he shifted
his weight to his weaker foot.
I wanted him to smell
the earth of the city that made us.

Brotherman,

the matter for ground big, e no fit enter boat.
As e de do you na so e de do me,
like say our life de waka go south.

No be say we no try make dem office oath
takers no spoil show. But wetin go be go still be.
The matter for ground big, e no fit enter boat.

Dem kill Dele Giwa, Saro-Wiwa and all the matter both
of them yarn. Brotherman, shey na like this we
go de look as our country de waka go south?

If you talk you go die. Mama Bornboy no fit clothe
him pickin. One president go jail, he drink tea
the matter for ground big, e no fit enter boat.

As oil de sell, big man belle de swell, na so we growth
de pafuka. Na how we take fall for our knee
be that as the land de waka go south.

For the protest, we don sing song, write poem and prose
join. The good thing be say all of us gree
say the matter for ground big, e no fit enter boat
everything for we country don waka go south.

Night

For several hours in my bed,
I thought about the bartender
who told me she thinks she would

die soon. The few times she was
by the coast the tide rose over
the levee in rage she was tempted

to drive into. She moved back
to the country for this. We were
strangers talking in a dwindling

bar and I hoped she would get
busy. I don't know more than
she told me. Last year she was

tortured in a room so white
it felt wrong to think of it
as a prison in Serbia where

she lived. I am not puzzled
by her delight to have come
home to her mother but my

father's return years after
his closet space was cleaned
out. For many days, I did not

know what to say to him.
I thought he would stay gone.

Island

I came to the lake with stories
from a fishwife who handed
my mother a breathing tilapia
with cooking instructions.
He came with his small laugh
and breakfast, which he did not share.
He said it was important to eat
before a fishing trip
because hunger is the reason
fishes are baited. This was how he said
my mother, who couldn't kill a fish
but continued to feed it in a glass bowl,
was a fool. I did not argue
with my father who as a boy
walked the streets with his empty
stomach; how can he imagine
a suffering greater than hunger?
When he bit his sandwich,
he had the widened eyes
of the boy he still carries inside him.
We did not return with a catch
though the worms were nibbled
off the hook. My father and I walked
back to his car in the silence of baited fools.

Backwards

I promise to not return
if this city won't meet
me with warmth. I do
not care for its women
and their brief love. I have
no sympathy for the woman
at the post office who mailed
her husband a love letter
addressed to another. Fuck
this city and its muddy lattes.
If I knew the woman in my
arms were married, I wouldn't
have reached for the music
in her mouth. From now on
I will board the first train to work.
I will take a rear facing seat for
a chance that the train might travel
backwards into the city of my youth.
You will be waiting with the anger
that burned my book of sonnets. And
I will have nothing to offer you
besides the unsweetened tea
that I have come to like.
I love you is as true as a train
traveling into the past. I am
reaching beyond my natural
abilities, like the woman at
the post office reaching
into the collection box for
a letter she sent decades ago.

Idris Dead

It has been eight years since he died,
and I admit to moving through the world
like it's a dark room. I left the country,
but the seas didn't drown the voices
of mourners saying he'd want me to go
on living. I have tried to forget the fever
of the night his eyes opened briefly before
they shut again. I have tried to make
a new life. When I lived by the coast,
I went to watch ships depart. I listened
for their horns, which may as well
be the last trumpet. I called my uncle's
name across the ocean, but the dead did not
speak over water. I was afraid I'll always
be alone. I moved to a village too small
to hide anything but they do not know
my dead. I shout their names at the hills
and it echoes through the woods like
it will go on ringing for many years.

4'33"

After Kei Miller

began with a pause,
the conductor's baton
hung still in midair like
a magic trick. The silence
broken by a man's cry
for his money back lasted
four minutes. His wife
weeping beside him said
she was leaving him. His
rage walked out of him, he held
her hands as she gathered
her coat and purse. Another
woman sang a lullaby over
the phone in low tone, she
promised to be home within
the hour. When the silence
resumed, she was gone.
The conductor bowed.
The composer explained
the work is comprised
of the random noises
in the hall by listeners.
After all, his intention
was to abolish prejudice
between music and noise.
Many of us sitting
still in our chairs
have forgotten how
much time has passed

as we waited. Our lives
could have gone past
a hundred years in one
night and we would not
have noticed.

Nomad

Alligator peppers stewing in a pot will make anyone cry. A tear for my father
Bent over his bowl in a shack on the land his father cultivated. See him
Cutting his trees. I always see him like that, even now that he has worked a
Deal that allowed him back in the house with my mother who won't cook him
Eggs for dinner. My father who can't farm or bring water to a boil but
Fought my mother over food and gossip. A tear for all the years I spent
Gathering news of his whereabouts. He left on Sunday. His leaving made our
House like a barren field over which a hawk caws. I saw him in the market.
I saw him by the lake where I lacked the courage to stop him on the
Jetty. I could have asked why he hurt me so, but I went on not
Knowing how to reconcile a father and a son. A tear for my mother who endured
Long years without word. She waited with me in a house falling apart on
Mango street. I thought it was a bad omen to wait until we are visited with
News. I left the country but dreamt of the house with its wide windows
Open. I stood outside and watched the hawk disappear into the wall. What
Purpose does a dream serve a son without his mother? To whom does he take his
Questions in a new country? Every man looks like my father from afar. Until I
Reach them and they are someone else's father. I have met doctors who asked me to
Share my sorrows. I always hesitate because I fear they pretend they can
Teach me to forgive my father. I don't want to. I only seek to
Understand what he left behind. I cannot mend my father. I cannot
Vouch for my interpretation of the dream with the hawk beating its
Wings against the wall. I thought it meant the wall was my father. A huge
X scrawled on the door to mean no access. I must now go into the
Years ahead. All the effort towards knowledge of my father's life comes to
Zero. A tear for time spent without resolution. A tear for my father.

Embers

My homeland was
this house
in the city.
What's left?

My homeland
was mortally
wounded.

What we swore to
uphold no longer
exists. Everyone
has died, or gone
away. That's all
I will say.

Unmastered

An inhabited house
with its furniture intact.

The photo frames on the wall,
the present lives of the people

who lived inside. Outside—
the senescent hibiscus petals

hanging low, the hydrangeas
outlived by weeds. The fence
and the rusty iron of its gate.

Outside—the neglected road,
cracked asphalt. Follow

the road to the school,
but there is no school. Stained

walls, charred bricks.
Outside—the flattened land,

then the obeche tall enough
to shelter. Then the network

of roots and canopy. Imagine
the land without the conflicts.

Outside—the field in the rain,
children jumping ropes.

Notes

"2000 Blacks" is from "2000 Blacks Got to Be Free" by Fela Kuti and Roy Ayers.

"Refuge" borrows a phrase from Tade Ipadeola's "The Sahara Testaments" and the 2006 movie *Blood Diamond*.

"Justice" refers to jungle justice, specifically the mob killing of four students in Aluu, Rivers State, Nigeria.

"Kalakuta Show" takes its title from Fela Kuti's album of the same title. The poem is after Fela Kuti's "Unknown Soldiers" and "Coffin for Head of State."

"4'33"" takes its title from John Cage's composition of the same title.

"Embers" is an erased poem from a chapter of *Embers* by Sandor Marai, translated by Carol Brown Janeway.

Acknowledgments

My thanks to the editors of the following journals and magazines in which these poems have appeared, sometimes in different versions, or with different titles:

> *A Longhouse*: "Noun" and "Heritage Park"; *Evergreen*: "Backwards"; *New England Review*: "Commutative Properties of Black Bodies"; *Poetry*: "Badagry."

I am grateful for the support of the Creative Writing Program at the University of Wisconsin–Madison, the Wallace Stegner Fellowship at Stanford University, the Olive B. O'Connor Fellowship at Colgate University, and the Elizabeth George Foundation.

I'm immensely thankful to my mentors and teachers: Amy Quan Barry, Amaud Jamaul Johnson, Jesse Lee Kercheval, Beth Nguyen, Patrick Phillips, A. Van Jordan, Louise Glück, Peter Balakian, and Jennifer Brice.

Gratitude to my friends who have shown up for me since the beginning of my journey as a writer. Ibukun Adeeko, Gbenga Adesina, Nurain Oladeji, Jubril Badmos, Servio Gbadamosi, Noah Oladele, Jide Salawu, Opeyemi Rasak-Oyadiran, Adedayo Agarau, Hauwa Shaffi Nuhu, Afeeya Ansong, Honora Ankong, Maggie Schenk, Xan Forrest, Wale Fadoju, Alessandra Occhiolini, Lena Crown, Damilare Omole, TaNia Donatto, Melissa Doty, Tosin Gbogi, Katherine Ho, Diana Khong, Fatima Oyetunji, Louise Ly, Dana Cypress, Ariel Martino, and Melissa Wallace.

I'm grateful to my friends from the UW–Madison writing program for being the helpful community they were. Thank you, Mishka Kabel Ligot for all your help. Thank you, Gabriella Balza for friendship;

Alison Thumel for our time together in Madison and Oakland; Adrienne Chung for energy that never tires. Thank you to Gabriel Louis and CJ for the best of times. I'm grateful to Clemonce Heard for helping me write this book and reading every draft of it. I'm thankful to Danie and Tim Shokoohi for their help.

I'm thankful to everyone who has been in a workshop with me, especially Jackson Holbert and Austin Araujo.

I'm grateful to my sister who has saved me many times with love. I'm grateful to my mother for her faith in me. Thank you to my father.

To my brother in heaven, Richard Anyah, for whom I couldn't write an elegy, so I wrote a book. Every poem is for you. Mo dúpẹ́.

I'm grateful to everyone who contributed to the book in any way. I apologize for any names that have slipped my memory.